Facilitator's Guide

HOW THE
Brain Learns
Mathematics

Facilitator's Guide

HOW THE
Brain Learns
Mathematics

David A. Sousa

CORWIN PRESS
A SAGE Company
Thousand Oaks, CA 91320

For information:

Corwin Press
A SAGE Company
2455 Teller Road
Thousand Oaks, California 91320
www.corwinpress.com

SAGE India Pvt. Ltd.
B 1/I 1 Mohan Cooperative Industrial Area
Mathura Road, New Delhi 110 044
India

SAGE Ltd.
1 Oliver's Yard
55 City Road
London EC1Y 1SP
United Kingdom

SAGE Asia-Pacific Pte. Ltd.
33 Pekin Street #02-01
Far East Square
Singapore 048763

Printed in the United States of America

ISBN: 978-1-4129-6590-3

This book is printed on acid-free paper.

08 09 10 11 12 10 9 8 7 6 5 4 3 2 1

Acquisitions Editor:	Robert D. Clouse
Editorial Assistant:	Jessica Bergmann
Production Editor:	Melanie Birdsall
Typesetter:	C&M Digitals (P) Ltd.
Proofreader:	Cheryl Rivard
Cover Designer:	Anthony Paular

Contents

About the Author   vii

Introduction   ix
   How to Use This Guide   ix
   Additional Resources for Facilitators   ix

Chapter-by-Chapter Study Guide:
   How the Brain Learns Mathematics by David A. Sousa   1

Introduction   1
   Summary   1
   Supplemental Information   2
   Discussion Questions   3

Chapter 1. Developing Number Sense   3
   Summary   3
   Supplemental Information   6
   Discussion Questions   6
   Activity   6
      Subitizing Versus Counting   6
   Journal Writing   7

Chapter 2. Learning to Calculate   7
   Summary   7
   Supplemental Information   9
   Discussion Questions   9
   Activity   9
      Multiplying While Talking   9
   Journal Writing   10

Chapter 3. Reviewing the Elements of Learning   10
   Summary   10
   Supplemental Information   14
   Discussion Questions   15
   Activity   15
      Demonstrating the Capacity
      Limit of Working Memory   15
   Journal Writing   16
   Activity   16
      Demonstrating the Primacy-Recency Effect 16
   Journal Writing   17

Chapter 4. Teaching Mathematics to
the Preschool and Kindergarten Brain   **17**
    Summary   17
    Supplemental Information   19
    Discussion Questions   19
    Activity   20
        Practicing a More Logical Counting System   20
    Journal Writing   20

Chapter 5. Teaching Mathematics
to the Preadolescent Brain   **20**
    Summary   20
    Supplemental Information   22
    Discussion Questions   22
    Activity   23
        Understanding the Environmental
            Influences on the Preadolescent Brain   23
    Journal Writing   24
    Activities   24
        Practicing Lattice Multiplication   24
        Preadolescent Brain Bingo   25
    Journal Writing   25

Chapter 6. Teaching Mathematics to the Adolescent Brain   **26**
    Summary   26
    Supplemental Information   29
    Discussion Questions   30
    Activity   31
        Planning a Layered Curriculum Unit   31
    Journal Writing   31

Chapter 7. Recognizing and Addressing
Mathematics Difficulties   **31**
    Summary   31
    Supplemental Information   34
    Discussion Questions   34
    Activity   35
        Alleviating Math Anxiety   35
    Journal Writing   35

Chapter 8. Putting It All Together: Planning
Lessons in PreK–12 Mathematics   **37**
    Summary   37
    Supplemental Information   38
    Discussion Questions   38
    Activity   39
        Planning an Activity for Multiple Intelligences 39
    Journal Writing   39

Workshop Evaluation Form   **41**

About the Author

David A. Sousa, EdD, is an international educational consultant. He has made presentations at national conventions of educational organizations and has conducted workshops on brain research and science education in hundreds of school districts and at colleges and universities across the United States, Canada, Europe, Asia, and Australia.

Dr. Sousa has a bachelor of science degree in chemistry from Massachusetts State College at Bridgewater, a master of arts degree in teaching science from Harvard University, and a doctorate from Rutgers University. His teaching experience covers all levels. He has taught high school science, served as a K–12 director of science, and was Supervisor of Instruction for the West Orange, New Jersey, schools. He then became superintendent of the New Providence, New Jersey, public schools. He has been an adjunct professor of education at Seton Hall University and a visiting lecturer at Rutgers University. He was president of the National Staff Development Council in 1992.

Dr. Sousa has edited science books and published numerous books and articles in leading educational journals on staff development, science education, and brain research. He has received awards from professional associations and school districts for his commitment and contributions to research, staff development, and science education. He received the Distinguished Alumni Award and an honorary doctorate in education from Bridgewater (Massachusetts) State College.

Dr. Sousa is a member of the Cognitive Neuroscience Society. He has appeared on the NBC *Today* show and on National Public Radio to discuss his work with schools using brain research. He makes his home in South Florida.

Introduction

This facilitator's guide is a companion for *How the Brain Learns Mathematics*, by David A. Sousa. It is designed to accompany the study of the book and provide assistance to group facilitators, such as school leaders, professional development coordinators, peer coaches, team leaders, mentors, and professors. Along with a summary of each chapter in the book, David A. Sousa has provided supplemental information, chapter discussion questions, activities, and journal writing prompts. For facilitators who conduct workshops, a sample workshop evaluation form is also included.

When using the guide during independent study, focus on the summaries and discussion questions.

For small study groups, the facilitator should guide the group through the chapter work.

For small- or large-group workshops, the facilitator should create an agenda by selecting activities and discussion starters from the chapter summary and discussion questions that meet the group's goals and guide the group through the learning process.

Additional Resources for Facilitators

Corwin Press also offers a free 16-page resource titled *Tips for Facilitators* that includes practical strategies and tips for guiding a successful meeting. The information in this resource describes different professional development opportunities, the principles of effective professional development, some characteristics of an effective facilitator, the responsibilities of the facilitator, and useful ideas for powerful staff development. *Tips for Facilitators* is available for free download at the Corwin Press Web site (www.corwinpress.com, under "Resources/Tips for Facilitators").

Chapter-by-Chapter Study Guide

How the Brain Learns Mathematics

by David A. Sousa

Summary

- Human beings are born with some remarkable capabilities. One is language. Toddlers can carry on running conversations without the benefit of direct instruction. Another innate talent is number sense—the ability to determine the number of objects in a small collection, to count, and to perform simple addition and subtraction, also without direct instruction.

- Why do so many children have difficulty learning mathematics in school? One reason is that spoken language and number sense are survival skills; abstract mathematics is not. In schools, we present complicated procedures to a brain that was first designed for survival in the African savanna. Human culture and society have changed a lot in the last 5,000 years, but the human brain has not.

- Thanks to modern imaging devices that can look inside the living brain, we can see which cerebral circuits are called into play when the brain tackles a task for which it has limited innate capabilities. The fact that the human brain can rise to this challenge is testimony to its remarkable ability to assess its environment and make calculations that can safely land humans on the moon and send a space probe to a planet hundreds of millions of miles away.

- The 2005 National Assessment of Educational Progress (NAEP) mathematics tests revealed that more than 39 percent of twelfth-grade students fell below the proficient level in basic mathematics skills. For fourth graders, the average score was three points higher in 2005 than in 2003, and for eighth graders, the average score was one point higher, on a 0 to 500-point scale. These increases were barely significant.
- Explanations for this poor performance include: (1) learning mathematics is difficult because it is so abstract and requires more logical and ordered thinking; (2) the various symbols used in mathematics make it similar to tackling a foreign language; and (3) while only a few students are really developmentally incapable of handling mathematics, the poor performance stems mainly from inadequate instruction sparked by the so-called "math wars."
- The National Council of Teachers of Mathematics (NCTM) published the *Principles and Standards for School Mathematics* in 2000, proposing five process standards and five content standards for PreK through Grade 12 mathematics instruction (NCTM, 2000). In 2006, NCTM released Curriculum Focal Points, which identifies three important mathematical topics at each level, PreK through Grade 8, described as "cohesive clusters of related knowledge, skills, and concepts," which form the necessary foundation for understanding concepts in higher-level mathematics. The publication is intended to bring more coherence to the very diverse mathematics curricula currently in use.
- This book discusses brain research that relates to teaching and learning, especially as it applies to learning mathematics. Some recent research findings are challenging long-held beliefs about how the brain processes arithmetic and mathematical operations. Mathematics educators should consider whether the curriculum topics and instructional strategies they select are consistent with these research findings.
- The book is not meant to be a source book for mathematics activities for PreK through Grade 12. Rather, it is meant to suggest instructional approaches that are compatible with what cognitive neuroscience is telling us about how the brain deals with numbers and mathematical relationships. This book is designed to help the teacher decide which of those books and activities are likely to be effective in light of current research.

Supplemental Information

Reports on student achievement in mathematics are mixed. Elementary and middle school scores are improving, while high school scores are level. According to the National Assessment of Educational Progress, the average score on the 2007 assessment for fourth graders has increased 27 points and the average score for eighth graders has increased 19 points since the first assessment in 1991. Between 2005 and 2007, fourth-grade scores rose two points and eighth-grade scores rose three points.

In high schools, the news about U.S. student achievement in mathematics continues to be disturbing. According to the Manhattan Institute for Policy Research, one in three students who enter college must repeat major parts of high school mathematics in order to enroll in courses such as College Algebra or Elementary Statistics. Also, the achievement gaps between white and minority students have generally not narrowed much over the years.

High schools have usually offered high-powered mathematics courses to those students preparing for college. But in this increasingly technological world, all students should graduate from high school with a strong grasp of basic mathematical concepts. Clearly, steps must be taken to make elementary and secondary school mathematics a challenging yet achievable experience for all students.

One way to make mathematics more interesting and meaningful to all students is to relate mathematical operations to the real world and minimize boring rote memorization of procedures. Mathematical influences can readily be discussed through topics such as, How do crude oil prices affect gasoline prices? and How do scientists measure global warming? Another way is to show how mathematics is used in other subject areas, such as economics, science, geography, and history. There are examples throughout this book on how to make mathematics meaningful.

Discussion Questions

1. What is innate number sense?
2. What reasons are given to explain why so many students do not do well on national tests of mathematics achievement?
3. How has the National Council of Teachers of Mathematics (NCTM) tried to deal with the wide diversity in mathematics curriculum and instructional strategies?

Chapter 1. Developing Number Sense

Summary

- Just a few months after birth, babies can already notice the constancy of objects and detect differences in numerical quantities, an ability known as *numerosity*. They also develop their innate number sense, the ability to recognize that something has changed in a small collection when, without that person's knowledge, an object has been added or removed from the collection. Number sense does not mean that we all can be great in mathematics. But it does mean that most of us have the potential to be a lot better at arithmetic and mathematics than we think. Some animals also have number sense.

- Contemporary research on number sense dramatically undermines Jean Piaget's views of 50 years ago. He believed that children did not possess number sense nor were they able to grasp the concept of number conservation—the idea that rearranging items in a collection does not change their number—until about five years of age. He also suggested that children do not develop a conceptual understanding of arithmetic until they are seven or eight years of age. Researchers today recognize that many of Piaget's experimental procedures with children were flawed, thus leading to erroneous conclusions. The ability of infants to acquire number concepts grows rapidly within their first year of life.

- Recognizing the number of objects in a small collection is part of innate number sense. It requires no counting because the numerosity is identified in an instant—a process called *subitizing*. When the number in a collection exceeds the limits of subitizing, counting becomes necessary. Recent brain scan studies indicate that subitizing is a primitive cerebral process, while counting involves more sophisticated operations. Subitizing may well be the developmental prerequisite skill necessary to learn counting.

- There are two types of subitizing: perceptual and conceptual. Perceptual subitizing involves recognizing a number without using other mathematical processes. It helps children separate collections of objects into single units and connect each unit with only one number word, thus developing the process of counting. Conceptual subitizing allows one to know the number of a collection by recognizing a familiar pattern, such as the spatial arrangement of dots on the faces of dice or on domino tiles. It helps young children develop the abstract number and arithmetic strategies they will need to master counting. Those children who cannot conceptually subitize will have problems learning basic arithmetic processes.

- By the age of 30 months, most children understand that counting is an abstract procedure that applies to all kinds of visual and auditory objects. By the age of three, most children recognize that there are separate words to describe the quantity of something; that is, they answer the question of "how many." For the young mind, counting is a complex process that uses a one-to-one principle. It involves saying number words in the correct sequence while systematically assigning a number word to each object being counted. Eventually, children recognize that the last number in the counting sequence tells them the total amount of objects in the collection, a concept known as the cardinal principle. Students who do not attain the cardinal principle will be delayed in their ability to add and subtract with meaning.

- The Western language systems for saying numbers pose more problems for children learning to count than do Asian languages. The Western systems are harder to keep in temporary memory, make the acquisition of counting and the conception of base 10 more difficult, and slow down calculation. No one realistically expects that Western counting systems will be modified to resemble the Asian model. But educators should at least be aware of these significant language problems, especially when they are comparing the test results in mathematics of Asian-speaking and English-speaking elementary students.

- Humans possess an internal number line that offers a limited degree of intuition about numbers. It deals with only positive integers and their quantitative relationship to each other. This probably explains why we have no intuition regarding other numbers that modern mathematicians use, such as negative integers, fractions, or irrational numbers. These entities remain difficult for the average person because they do not correspond to any natural category in our brain. Small positive integers make such sense to our innate sense of numerosity that even four-year-olds can comprehend them. But the other entities make no such natural connection. To understand them, we have to construct mental models that provide understanding.

- The human brain comprehends numerals as a quantity, not as words. Automatically and unconsciously, numerical symbols are converted almost instantly to an internal quantity. Moreover, the conversion includes an automatic orientation of numbers in space, small ones to the left and large ones to the right. Comprehending numbers, then, is a reflex action that is deeply rooted in our brains, resulting in an immediate attribution of meaning to numbers.

- The expanded view of number sense includes a wide array of abilities related to manipulating and interpreting mathematical operations. Mathematics educators recognize that both formal and informal instruction can enhance number sense development prior to entering school.

- Sharon Griffin's model suggests that the development of number sense goes through three major phases: recognizing objects in a collection, creating number words to communicate an exact count to others, and creating numerical symbols and operational signs to manipulate numerical expressions.

- Number sense can be considered the innate beginnings of mathematical intelligence as described by Howard Gardner. But the extent to which it becomes an individual's major talent still rests with the type and strength of the genetic input and the environment in which the individual grows and learns.

Supplemental Information

Although some Piaget-oriented psychologists still question whether human beings possess number sense, the research findings from cognitive neuroscience in support of an innate number sense are very convincing. Rather than hanging on to outdated ideas about how limited youngsters might be in processing numerical quantities, we should welcome the research findings. They imply that most students have an inherent capability to be successful at basic and concrete arithmetic operations.

Discussion Questions

1. Describe number sense. What are its capabilities and limitations?
2. How does our current understanding of number sense compare with Piaget's beliefs about a child's ability to deal with numbers and arithmetic operations?
3. Describe subitizing and its two types.
4. How does a child's sense of counting develop?
5. How does a child's native language affect learning to count?
6. Describe the internal number line. What are its capabilities and limitations?
7. What kinds of abilities are included in the expanded view of number sense? To what degree can these abilities be taught?
8. How does number sense relate to Gardner's description of logical/mathematical intelligence?

Activity

● *Subitizing Versus Counting*

Time: 15 minutes
Materials: *How the Brain Learns Mathematics*, an overhead transparency (or PowerPoint slide) similar to Figure 1.2 on page 14 of the text, chart paper, markers

The purpose of this activity is to help the participants recognize the difference between subitizing (knowing number without counting) and counting. This is often a difficult concept for some to grasp, but it is important for understanding the difference between an innate capability (subitizing) and a learned process (counting).

Make sure that the participants have their textbook closed. Put the **covered** transparency on the overhead projector. Quickly reveal the top two boxes (Box A and Box B) for only a second or two. Ask the participants to jot down how many circles they saw in each box, without talking to each other. Now reveal the bottom two boxes (Box C and Box D) for about four seconds. Once again, ask the participants to independently write down how many circles were in each box. On chart paper (or overhead transparency), write down the group's answers for each of the four boxes.

Ask the participants to get up and walk across the room, find a partner, and alternate sharing their explanation for the group's answers to the number of circles in each one of the four boxes. Why do the results for Boxes C and D vary so much?

Journal Writing

1. (Complete the following statement.) When I was in elementary and high school, learning mathematics for me was _____ because _____.
2. Explain how subitizing differs from counting.

Chapter 2. Learning to Calculate

Summary

- Counting up to small quantities comes naturally to children. Either spontaneously or by imitating their peers, they begin to solve simple arithmetic problems based on counting, with or without words. Their first excursion into calculation occurs when they add two sets by counting them both on their fingers. Gradually, they learn to add without using their fingers and, by the age of five, demonstrate an understanding of *commutativity* of addition (the rule that $a + b$ is always equal to $b + a$). One thing is certain: the human brain has serious problems with calculations. Nothing in its evolution prepared it for the task of memorizing dozens of multiplication facts nor for carrying out the multistep operations required for two-digit subtraction. Our ability to approximate numerical quantities may be embedded in our genes, but dealing with exact symbolic calculation can be an error-prone ordeal.
- Conceptual structures about numbers develop early and allow children to experiment with calculations in their preschool years. They quickly master many addition and subtraction strategies, carefully selecting those that are best suited for a particular problem. As they apply their algorithms, they mentally determine how much time it took them to make the calculation and the likelihood that the result is correct. Gradually, they revise their collection of strategies and retain those that are most appropriate for

each numerical problem. Exposure at home to activities involving arithmetic plays an important role in this process by offering children new algorithms and by providing them with a variety of rules for choosing the best strategy. The dynamic process of creating, refining, and selecting algorithms for basic arithmetic is established in most children before they reach kindergarten.

- Exactly how number structures develop in young children is not completely understood. However, in recent years, research in cognitive neuroscience has yielded sufficient clues about brain development to the point that researchers have devised a timeline of how number structures evolve in the brain in the early years. There are three core assumptions about how the development of conceptual structures progresses.

  1. Major reorganization in children's thinking occurs around the age of five years when cognitive structures that were created in earlier years are integrated into a hierarchy.

  2. Important changes in cognitive structures occur about every two years during the development period. The ages of 4, 6, 8, and 10 years are used in this model because they represent the midpoint of the development phases (ages 3 to 5, 5 to 7, 7 to 9, and 9 to 11).

  3. This developmental progression is typical for about 60 percent of children in a modern, developed culture. Thus, about 20 percent of children will develop at a faster rate, while about 20 percent will progress at a slower rate.

- The mental processes required to perform multiplication are more involved and somewhat different from the innate processes used for addition and subtraction, which were sufficiently adequate to allow our ancestors to survive. As a result, humans need to devise learning tools to help them conquer multiplication.

- Preschool children use their innate but limited notions of numerosity to develop intuitive counting strategies that will help them understand and measure larger quantities. But they never get to continue following this intuitive process. The way we most often teach the multiplication tables is counterintuitive. Usually, we start with the one times table and work our way up to the ten times table. Taught step by step in this fashion results in 100 (10 × 10) separate facts to be memorized.

- Pattern interference also makes it difficult for our memory to keep addition and multiplication facts separate. For example, it takes us longer to realize that 2 × 3 = 5 is wrong than to realize that 2 × 3 = 7 is false because the first result would be correct under addition. Our brain has evolved to equip us with necessary survival skills. Rudimentary counting is easy because of our abilities to use language and to denote a one-to-one correspondence with finger manipulation. But our brains are not equipped to manipulate the arithmetic facts needed to do precise calculations, such as multiplication, because these operations were not essential to our species' survival. Consequently, to do multiplication and precise calculations, we have to recruit mental circuits that developed for quite different reasons.

- Humans are able to extend their intuitive number sense to a capacity to perform exact arithmetic by recruiting the language areas of our brain. Yet despite this seeming cooperation between the language and mathematical reasoning areas of the brain, it is still important to remember that these two cerebral areas are anatomically separate and distinct. Teachers, then, should not assume that students who have difficulty with language processing will necessarily encounter difficulties in arithmetic computation, and vice versa.

Supplemental Information

How and when to introduce the multiplication tables is still a matter of controversy. The highly regarded Singapore Mathematics Syllabus does include the multiplication tables, but it introduces them at earlier grade levels than NCTM recommends in its *Curriculum Focal Points*. The challenge for the teacher is that primary students at the beginning of the school year arrive at different levels of competence in their exposure and mastery of the multiplication tables. Successful learning of multiplication facts is more likely to occur if they can be incorporated into lesson activities without rote memorization and endless drills.

Discussion Questions

1. Describe how conceptual structures about numbers progress in 4-, 6-, 8-, and 10-year-old students.
2. Why does the human brain have such difficulty when encountering multiplication processes?
3. What role does memory play in carrying out multiplication?
4. If you had to teach multiplication facts to primary grade students, how would you do it? How would you justify your approach?
5. What is associative memory, and how can it cause problems when students are learning the multiplication tables?
6. How does language help or hinder learning multiplication?

Activity

● *Multiplying While Talking*

Time: 5–10 minutes
Materials: Paper, pencil

The purpose of this activity is to recognize the interrelationships between the regions of the brain that process language and those that deal with numerical operations. Ask the participants to write down a pair of two-digit numbers that they are going to multiply. The numbers should be written in the following multiplication format:

$$\begin{array}{r} AB \\ \times\ CD \\ \hline \end{array}$$

Ask them to multiply the two numbers quickly and accurately, and to estimate about how long it took them to complete the task. They should write down that approximate time next to their answer.

Now ask them to write down a different pair of two-digit numbers in the same format. This time, tell them to start multiplying the numbers while quietly and simultaneously reciting the alphabet. Once again, they should estimate the time it took them to complete the multiplication, and write down that time next to the answer.

When everyone is done, ask them to walk across the room and, working in pairs, review their results with a partner. They should discuss any significant differences in the time it took to solve the two problems and decide on how they would explain these differences. Provide an opportunity for the participants to share their thoughts with the entire group.

Journal Writing

What are three things I learned about how the young brain learns to calculate?

Chapter 3. Reviewing the Elements of Learning

Summary

- Teachers want their students to remember forever what they have learned in class. But this is not often the case. The more teachers know about memory systems, the more likely they are to plan lessons that will result in greater retention.
- There are two temporary memories, immediate memory and working memory. Immediate memory is a place where we put information briefly until we make a decision on how to dispose of it. Immediate memory operates subconsciously or consciously and holds data for up to about 30 seconds. The individual's experiences determine the degree of the information's importance. If the information is of little or no importance within this time frame, it drops out of the temporary memory system.

- Working memory is a place of limited capacity where we can build, take apart, or rework ideas for eventual disposal or storage somewhere else. When something is in working memory, it generally captures our focus and demands our attention. Working memory can handle only a few items at one time, from two to seven, depending on the learner's age. It is possible to increase the number of items within the functional capacity of working memory through a process called chunking. In arithmetic, chunking occurs when the young child's mind quickly recognizes that both 3 + 1 + 1 and 3 + 2 equal 5. The implication of these findings is that teachers should consider capacity limits when deciding on the amount of information they present in a lesson. Less is more.

- Working memory is a temporary memory and can deal with items for only a limited time. For preadolescents, that time is more likely to be 5 to 10 minutes and for adolescents and adults, 10 to 20 minutes. For focus to continue, there must be some *change* in the way the individual is dealing with the item. If something else is not done with the item, it is likely to fade from working memory. The implication here is that teachers should consider these working memory time limits when deciding on the flow of their lessons. Shorter is better.

- Any new learning is more likely to be retained if the learner has adequate time to process and reprocess it, called *rehearsal*. Time is a critical component of rehearsal. Initial rehearsal occurs when the information first enters working memory. If the learner cannot attach sense or meaning, and if there is no time for further processing, then the new information is likely to be lost. Providing sufficient time to go beyond the initial processing to secondary rehearsal allows the learner to review the information, to make sense of it, to elaborate on the details, and to assign value and relevance, thus increasing significantly the chance of retention.

- Rote rehearsal is used when the learner needs to remember and store information exactly as it is entered into working memory. This is not a complex strategy, but it is necessary to learn information or a cognitive skill in a specific form or an exact sequence. We use rote rehearsal to remember a poem, the lyrics and melody of a song, telephone numbers, steps in a procedure, and the multiplication tables.

- Elaborative rehearsal is used not when it is necessary to store information exactly as learned but when it is more important to associate the new learnings with prior learnings to detect relationships. Students use rote rehearsal to memorize mathematical facts but use elaborative rehearsal to probe the deeper meanings and interrelationships of mathematical concepts.

- Working memory uses two criteria to decide which information gets stored, sense and meaning. Sense refers to whether the learner can understand the mathematical content on the basis of experience. Does it "fit" into what the learner already knows about numbers and arithmetic operations? Meaning refers to whether the item is relevant to the learner. For what purpose should the learner remember it? Meaning is a very personal thing and is greatly influenced by an individual's experiences. The same item can have great meaning for one student and none for another.

- Information can be stored in different ways. Long-term memory can be divided into two major types, declarative memory and nondeclarative memory. Declarative memory describes the remembering of names, facts, music, and objects. Declarative memory can be further divided into episodic memory and semantic memory. Episodic memory refers to the conscious memory of events in our own life history. It helps us identify the time and place when an event happened and gives us a sense of self. Semantic memory is knowledge of facts and data that may not be related to any event. A student later recalling the Pythagorean theorem is using semantic memory; remembering his experiences in the classroom when he learned it is episodic memory.

- Nondeclarative memory describes all memories that are not declarative memories; that is, they are memories that can be used for things that cannot be declared or explained in any straightforward manner. Of particular interest to teachers of mathematics is the type of nondeclarative memory called procedural memory.

- Procedural memory refers to the learning of motor and cognitive skills and remembering *how* to do something, like riding a bicycle, driving a car, and tying a shoelace. As practice of the skills continues, these memories become more efficient and can be performed with little conscious thought or recall. The brain process shifts from *reflective* to *reflexive*.

- Procedural memory is enhanced by the repetition of rote rehearsal. That is the only way we can retain certain information, such as how to add a column of numbers. Because following a step-by-step procedure usually gives us the desired outcome, we can carry out the steps without much conscious input and without having a clue as to *why* we are doing them.

- In a learning episode, we tend to remember best that which comes first, and remember second best that which comes last. We remember least that which comes just past the middle of the episode. This common phenomenon is referred to as the primacy-recency effect (also known as the serial position effect). The implication here is that important new learning should be presented at the beginning of the lesson and rehearsed at the end.

- Practice may not make perfect, it makes permanent. We want to ensure that students practice the new learning correctly from the beginning. This guided practice is done in the presence of the teacher, who offers immediate and corrective feedback. When the practice is correct, the teacher can then assign independent practice (usually homework) in which the students can rehearse the skill on their own to enhance retention. Teachers should avoid giving students independent practice before guided practice because the students may unknowingly practice the skill or procedure incorrectly.

- Practicing a new learning during time periods that are very close together is massed practice. This produces fast learning, as when one mentally rehearses a multiplication table. Immediate memory is involved here, and the information can fade in seconds if it is not rehearsed quickly. Sustained practice over time is distributed practice and is the key to retention. If you want to remember a multiplication table later on, you will need to use it repeatedly over time. Thus, practice that is distributed over longer periods of time sustains meaning and consolidates the learnings into long-term storage in a form that will ensure accurate recall and applications in the future.

- Writing activities help students to learn a concept more effectively, organize ideas, and become active participants in their learning. They get involved in an active intellectual process in which they decide what is important and what is meaningful or relevant to them and gain self-understanding and confidence in dealing with their concerns.

- Although the genders have differed on test results in mathematics, researchers believe social context plays an important role. Differences in career choices, for instance, are due not to differing abilities in mathematics but to cultural factors, such as subtle but pervasive gender expectations that emerge in high school. This phenomenon is called stereotype threat and occurs when people believe they will be evaluated based on societal stereotypes about their particular group. Manipulating the way female students thought of themselves affects their performance on mathematics tests. Studies suggest that males and females on the whole have equal aptitude for mathematics and science.

- Learning style describes the ways and preferences an individual has when in a learning situation and seems to result from a combination of genetic predispositions and environmental influences. These styles include sensory preferences, hemispheric preference, intellectual preferences similar to Gardner's multiple intelligences, participation preferences, and sensing/intuitive preferences. These preferences can change temporarily if the situation requires it.

- Some researchers suggest that mathematicians view their subject from any one of three perspectives:
  1. Platonist—mathematics exists in an abstract plane, but the objects of mathematics that they study are as real as everyday life.
  2. Formalist—mathematics is only a game in which one manipulates symbols in accordance with precise formal rules. Mathematical objects such as numbers have no relation to reality.
  3. Intuitionist—mathematical objects are merely constructions of the human mind. Mathematics does not exist in the real world, but only in the brain of the mathematician who invents it.

Supplemental Information

Numerous studies that look at how we remember information continue to emphasize the importance of *meaning*. Although the brain occasionally remembers isolated trivia, most information is remembered because the learner has found meaning in it. This is a good time to remind participants that teachers spend an average of only about 10 percent of their lesson preparation time planning for meaning. That is why teachers continue to hear those annoying questions: "Why do we have to know this?" or "When will I ever use this?"

Meaning can come in many ways. One of the more successful ways for students to see meaning is through real-life applications. Whenever teachers can show the practical applications of mathematics, students are likely to see mathematics as relevant to their world and, thus, worth remembering.

Some secondary-school teachers of mathematics are frequent offenders of the "guided practice before independent practice" rule. They use much of the class time showing the students how to solve a problem or use a particular axiom or formula. As the class period draws to a close, they say, "Well, we didn't have time for you to try this out in class, but let me give you some problems to try at home tonight, and tomorrow we'll see how well you did." (If the participants in your study group are willing, you might just ask how many of them have been in this situation. Then ask how frequently it happens to them.)

As explained in the text (pages 62–63), the situation just described can be a recipe for disaster. If some students have not learned the solution or procedure correctly, then the independent practice at home will help make the *incorrect* learning permanent, because new learning gets consolidated into long-term memory during sleep! Now when these students discover at their next mathematics class that they have learned the procedure incorrectly, they are now faced with unlearning/relearning, a process that some frustrated students may just not undertake. It is important, then, to emphasize that, with very few exceptions, guided practice must occur before independent practice.

Discussion Questions

1. Describe the functions of immediate memory and working memory.
2. What are the capacity and time limits of working memory? What implications do these limits have for teaching and learning?
3. Explain initial and secondary rehearsal.
4. Explain rote and elaborative rehearsal. In what learning situation would you use one and not the other?
5. What criteria does the brain generally use to determine what information gets stored?
6. Explain the differences between declarative memory and non-declarative memory.
7. What is the primacy-recency effect? What implications does it have for teaching and learning?
8. Describe guided practice, independent practice, massed practice, and distributed practice. What does the old saying "Practice makes perfect" have to do with these strategies?
9. How would you explain the apparent gender differences that occur in mathematics achievement scores, whereby boys nearly always outperform girls?
10. What impact do learning styles have in learning mathematics?
11. What impact do teaching styles have in teaching mathematics?

Activity

- *Demonstrating the Capacity Limit of Working Memory*

Time: 5–10 minutes
Materials: Overhead projector, paper, pencil

This activity is designed to show that working memory has limits in the amount of information it can process at one time. Prepare in advance an overhead transparency (or PowerPoint slide) that looks like the following:

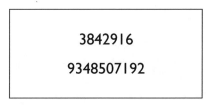

Place the **covered** transparency on the overhead projector. Ask the participants to focus on the screen and to commit to memory the number that you will reveal. Now uncover only the seven-digit number for seven seconds. (You can count "one Mississippi, two

Mississippi . . ."quietly to yourself.) Cover the number and ask the participants to write the number down. Then ask them to focus on the screen again and to remember the next number. Uncover the 10-digit number for seven seconds. Cover it and ask them to write down that number. How well did they do?

Organize the participants in pairs and have them discuss their results with their partners along with the implications this has for teaching and learning.

Journal Writing

How will I use my knowledge of the capacity limits of working memory when I plan my lessons?

Activity

● *Demonstrating the Primacy-Recency Effect*

Time: 20–30 minutes, with reading
Materials: Overhead projector, prepared transparencies (or PowerPoint slides), prepared worksheet, pencils, *How the Brain Learns Mathematics*

This entertaining activity is an excellent way to clearly demonstrate with data the power of the primacy-recency effect. Distribute to the participants a worksheet that looks like the "Retention Activity" example shown here. Tell the participants that you are going to show them a list of 10 common, everyday English words that are arranged in a vertical column. The list will be on the screen for only a few seconds. Their job is to memorize as many of the words as they can and their position on the list. When you turn off the projector, they are to write down as many words as they remember in the correct position. So, if they do not remember word three but remember word four, then it gets written on line 4.

Also tell them two important conditions: First, this is **not** a cooperative learning exercise. Each person works alone! Second, they are not to write down any words until the projector is turned off (or the list is completely covered).

Prepare in advance an overhead transparency (or PowerPoint slide) that looks like the list shown here. (Note: You can choose other

Retention Activity
1. _____
2. _____
3. _____
4. _____
5. _____
6. _____
7. _____
8. _____
9. _____
10. _____

words if you prefer, but keep them to no more than two syllables and be sure they are common items.)

Ask the participants to focus on the screen. Reveal the entire list for 14 seconds. Make sure you are not blocking anyone's view of any of the words. After 14 seconds, turn off the projector (or completely cover the list) and ask the participants to write down as many words as they remember in the correct position. **Remain quiet during this time so they are not distracted from their task.**

| CAR |
| TACK |
| LAMP |
| NEEDLE |
| PAPER |
| COIN |
| PILLOW |
| DESK |
| KNIFE |
| BOOT |

When the participants are finished, turn the projector on (or uncover the list) and ask them to put a check next to the words they remembered and wrote down in the correct position. Then, starting with the first word, ask those participants who got it correct to raise their hand. Count the hands and write that number on the transparency (or slide, if possible) next to that word. Do this for all 10 words.

Note that the highest number of words correctly remembered will be at the beginning of the list. There will be a significant drop off in correct answers around the sixth word. The second highest number of correct answers will be of the two or three words at the end of the list. This activity clearly demonstrates the primacy-recency effect.

Ask the participants to read (or reread) pages 61–63 of the text and to think about the implications of this effect for teaching and learning. Then get them up and moving around the room to find a partner. Each member of the pair takes about a minute to discuss one implication.

Journal Writing

How does my understanding of the primacy-recency effect affect the way I plan my lessons?

Chapter 4. Teaching Mathematics to the Preschool and Kindergarten Brain

Summary

- Preschoolers should learn mathematics because they already encounter curricular areas that include only a small amount of mathematics. Supplemental instruction would help make these areas more understandable. Many preschoolers experience difficulties with mathematics in their later years. This potential gap can be narrowed by including more mathematics at the preschool level. Preschoolers already possess number and geometry abilities ranging from counting objects to making shapes. Children use mathematical ideas in their everyday life and can develop surprisingly sophisticated mathematical knowledge. Preschool activities should extend these abilities.

- One of the first tasks of a preschool and kindergarten teacher is to determine the level of number sense that each student has already reached. Using assessment tests, a teacher can determine how far an individual student's number sense has progressed. The teacher can then use differentiated activities to develop the number sense for students of the same age who may be at different levels of competence.

- Subitizing is the ability to know the number of objects in a small collection without counting. Strengthening this skill should make learning to count easier for young students. The ability to subitize can be developed, and preschool and kindergarten teachers should consider incorporating activities that strengthen this capability in their young students. In activities that strengthen subitizing, teachers should use cards or objects with dot patterns and avoid using manipulatives, which could encourage counting.

- By the age of four, most children have mastered basic counting and can apply counting to new situations. Reciting number words in a fixed sequence is a natural outcome of our facility with language. And the principle of one-to-one correspondence is actually widespread in the animal kingdom. Once children learn to count using objects, the next challenge is to learn to count mentally without objects. Children who have been practicing activities that enhance visualization are likely to learn mental counting more easily because it is so heavily dependent on imagery. The next step is the realization that when two quantities are joined, counting can begin from the last number of one quantity rather than starting all over from one. This is called *counting on* and is an advanced strategy used by children to solve problems in addition.

- Asian children have a much easier time learning how to count because their language logically describes the counting sequence. Some early childhood researchers suggest trying out this approach with English-speaking children, using English counting words in a pattern similar to that used in some Asian languages. This method requires just 10 different words to count from 1 to 100 instead of the 28 English words needed for the traditional counting method. The numbers in this approach are not shorter or faster to say, but they make a lot more sense and help children get a deeper understanding of our base-10 system. Schools in North America where this has been used have not reported any significant confusion. Children will learn the traditional counting words without any instruction through their exposure to adults, television, and other media.

- Young children use sorting and classifying skills to organize their world. Both skills emerge around the age of three. As these skills develop, children begin to recognize the differences between plants and animals, day and night, and different geometric shapes. They enhance their number sense and their intuitive understandings about how to manipulate numbers during mathematical operations. As a result, they begin to apply logical thinking to the mathematical concepts they encounter. *Sorting* and *classifying* are terms that are often used synonymously, but they represent two separate levels of logical thinking. Sorting is a grouping task in which the student is told how the objects will be sorted. Classifying, however, requires students to discover how a given set of objects might be grouped. Unlike sorting tasks, the students are not told to put objects into groups based on a particular attribute. With classifying tasks, students must decide how the objects in each group might be alike.

Supplemental Information

Some educators still believe that the brain of a preschooler is not ready for learning mathematics skills. But the growing body of research refutes this notion. If the instruction builds on the child's innate number sense and capabilities to sort and classify, then the skills needed to understand and manipulate small numerical quantities can certainly be taught to most preschool and kindergarten students. Direct the participants to the **Resources** section of the text, which lists some Internet sites where many arithmetic activities for preschool and kindergarten students can be found.

Discussion Questions

1. Should preschoolers learn mathematics? Why or why not?
2. What are some of the areas and skills in mathematics that preschoolers and kindergartners should learn?
3. Describe some strategies that teachers can use to help young children build their subitizing skills.
4. Why do Asian children have an easier time learning to count than native English-speaking children?
5. What is the difference between sorting and classifying? Give an example of each.

6. Describe the four levels of sorting.
7. Describe the four levels of classifying.

Activity

● *Practicing a More
  Logical Counting System*

Time: 15–20 minutes, with reading
Materials: Paper, pencils, *How the Brain Learns Mathematics*

The purpose of this activity is to get the participants to think of counting words in a new format that mimics the counting system of some major Asian languages, such as Chinese and Japanese. Ask the participants to read "An Easier Counting System" on page 87 of the text, and to study the chart on page 88. Give them enough time to feel comfortable with the Asian-like counting system. When they have finished this task, ask them to close the text. Now ask them to write down on a piece of paper five two-digit numbers and to say each number to themselves using the system they just studied on page 88. However, they should **not** write down the counting words on the paper. Now ask them to take the paper with the five numbers with them as they get up, move across the room, and find a partner. They will then exchange the paper with their partner and take turns reading each of the five numbers aloud to their partner, using the Asian-like counting system. When completed, ask the pairs to discuss whether they believe this system can be of benefit to young children learning to count.

Journal Writing

What are two things I learned from this discussion that will help me in my teaching (or parenting)?

Chapter 5. Teaching Mathematics to the Preadolescent Brain

Summary

- The limbic area is largely involved in generating emotional responses. The emotional (and biologically older) system develops faster and matures much earlier than the frontal lobes. The limbic area is fully mature around the age of 10 to 12 years, but the frontal lobes mature closer to 22 to 24 years of age. Consequently, the emotional system is more likely to win the tug-of-war for control of behavior during the preadolescent years. What does this mean for preadolescents? Emotional messages guide the individual's behavior, including directing its attention to a learning situation. Specifically, emotion drives attention and attention drives learning. But even more important to understand is that emotional attention comes *before* cognitive recognition.

- Preadolescents are likely to respond emotionally to a learning situation much faster than responding rationally. Getting their attention for a lesson in mathematics means trying to find an emotional link to the day's learning objective. Whenever a teacher attaches a positive emotion to the mathematics lesson, it not only gets attention, but it also helps the students to see mathematics as having real-life applications.

- It is important to teach mathematics in a way that makes it meaningful for students. Recognizing that meaning is a criterion for long-term storage, teachers should *purposefully* plan for meaning in their lessons. For example, meaning can come through using multiple models and through cognitive closure.

- Preadolescents are primed for learning process skills. These process skills should include enhancing number sense, developing estimation skills, strategies that result in understanding the concept rather than rote memorization, and developing mathematical reasoning.

- Today's students have grown up in a visual world. They are surrounded by television, computer screens, movies, portable DVD players, and cell phones with screen images. Using visual tools in the mathematics classroom, then, makes a lot of sense. Graphic organizers are one type of visual tool that not only get students' attention but are also valuable devices for improving understanding, meaning, and retention.

- Students today have grown up with technology. Using new technologies involves time, effort, and a rethinking of instructional approaches. Studies indicate that teachers are still not using technology as often as students expect, nor in ways that students perceive as helpful. Why is technology not being used often in mathematics classes? Mathematics teachers say that a number of factors served to inhibit and encourage teachers to use technology in their mathematics classes.

- Teachers are sometimes torn between the enthusiasm for using technology in mathematical investigations and the cautions about undermining students' computational skills. Research studies show that, particularly in middle grade mathematics, technology can have positive effects on students' attitudes toward learning, on their confidence in their abilities to do mathematics, and on their motivation and time on task. Furthermore, technology use can help students make significant gains in mathematical achievement and conceptual understanding.

- Research studies also suggest that using technology for *nonroutine* applications, such as exploring number concepts and solving complex problems, leads students to greater conceptual understanding and higher achievement, whereas using technology for routine calculations does not. Students often perceive calculators as simply computational tools. But when they engage in mathematical exploration and problem solving with calculators, they broaden their perspective and see calculators as tools that can enhance their learning and understanding of mathematics.

Supplemental Information

One of the areas to emphasize in this chapter is the section on mathematical reasoning. It is through mathematical reasoning that students will be able to make the transition from arithmetic to algebra. Eighth graders continue to score poorly on national tests of multistep problems and algebra. The NCTM *Curriculum Focal Points* emphasize connections to algebra as early as kindergarten and support the development of algebraic reasoning through the elementary and middle school grades.

Algebraic reasoning builds on students' deep understanding of

- numbers and number relationships;
- functional relationships between numbers; and
- number property axioms, such as the associative, commutative, distributive principles, etc.

Researchers continue to be puzzled that many teachers of mathematics do not use all the technology available to them during instruction. Students today have grown up in a technology-rich culture. When properly used, technology can enrich, enhance, and support mathematics curriculum objectives at all grade levels.

Discussion Questions

1. Discuss the development of the preadolescent brain and the possible implications for learning mathematics.
2. Compare the development of the brain's limbic area to the development of the frontal lobes from birth to young adulthood.
3. What are some of the environmental factors influencing the preadolescent brain and what implications do they have for learning?
4. Describe cognitive closure. Explain whether you think this is an effective teaching strategy. Why or why not?

5. How would you design a lesson to develop and enhance number sense?
6. How would you design a lesson to develop estimating skills?
7. Explain the declarative-based approach to problem solving.
8. Why is it important to develop mathematical reasoning in preadolescents?
9. In what ways can teachers use technology to foster the learning and enjoyment of mathematics?

Activity

● *Understanding the Environmental Influences on the Preadolescent Brain*

Time: 20–30 minutes, with reading
Materials: *How the Brain Learns Mathematics*

The purpose of this activity is to discuss the various environmental factors that influence the developing brain. This is a round-robin-type activity where each participant becomes an "expert" in one group (the expert group) about a topic and then teaches it to other participants in a different group (the sharing group).

Expert groups. Organize the participants into six expert groups. Number the groups from 1 to 6. Ask everyone to open the text to page 102. There are six environmental factors described in Table 5.2. Group 1 will focus on the first factor (family units), Group 2 on the second factor (media), and so on through Group 6 (novelty). The task of each group is to discuss fully the environmental factor assigned to them and the implications this factor has for learning. Members can contribute other implications in addition to those in the text. The discussion should continue until each member of the group feels like an "expert" in that factor and its implications. Give the groups about 5–7 minutes for this task (or longer if you have particularly large groups).

Sharing groups. Now reorganize the participants into groups of six, so that there is one person from each of the expert groups in the newly formed sharing group. To start, the Group 1 expert explains to the rest of the group the first factor from Table 5.2 and its implications. The expert should allow time for questions and comments from the other group members. Then the Group 2 through Group 6 experts take their turn in numerical order to explain their factors and implications. If you have sharing groups with less than six experts, ask the group to read about and discuss those factors not represented by an expert.

When completed, ask if anyone would like to share thoughts or observations with the entire group.

Journal Writing

What are at least three implications from this activity that will have an impact on my teaching?

Activities

● *Practicing Lattice Multiplication*

Time: 15–20 minutes, with reading
Materials: Prepared worksheet, pencils, *How the Brain Learns Mathematics*

This activity provides participants an opportunity to practice lattice multiplication. Some may have already used this method, but it will be new to many of them. Ask the participants to open the text to page 122 and to read the section on lattice multiplication and to study the example in Figure 5.8.

Distribute a copy of the worksheet shown here to each participant.

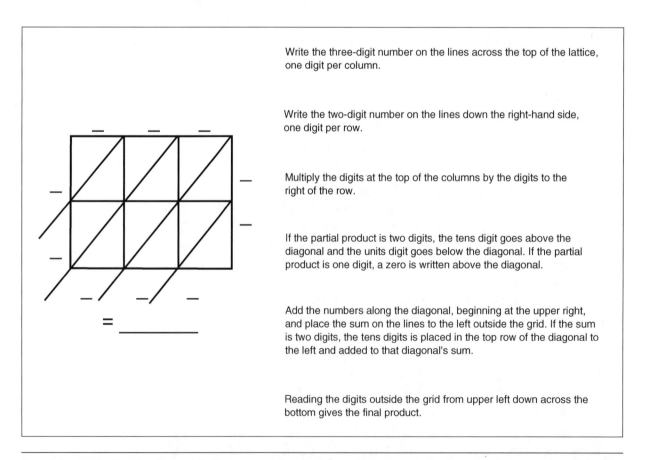

Write the three-digit number on the lines across the top of the lattice, one digit per column.

Write the two-digit number on the lines down the right-hand side, one digit per row.

Multiply the digits at the top of the columns by the digits to the right of the row.

If the partial product is two digits, the tens digit goes above the diagonal and the units digit goes below the diagonal. If the partial product is one digit, a zero is written above the diagonal.

Add the numbers along the diagonal, beginning at the upper right, and place the sum on the lines to the left outside the grid. If the sum is two digits, the tens digits is placed in the top row of the diagonal to the left and added to that diagonal's sum.

Reading the digits outside the grid from upper left down across the bottom gives the final product.

The participants can work either alone or in pairs, depending on their comfort level with the lattice process. Ask the participants to multiply a three-digit number by a two-digit number, using the lattice method. They can use the instructions on the worksheet for guidance. When completed, ask them to discuss with a partner the advantages and disadvantages of introducing this method of multiplication to preadolescents. Discuss the process with the entire group.

● *Preadolescent Brain Bingo*

Time: 20 minutes
Materials: Copies of the Preadolescent Brain Bingo game sheet for each participant

This activity is an excellent review of the chapter, using an amusing and physically active bingo-card format. Have the participants read the instructions on the Preadolescent Brain Bingo game sheets (see page 26 of this guide) as well as the information in the squares. Give them adequate time to review their notes and the chapter. Some participants like to become "experts" in a particular topic during the game.

After several minutes of review time, ask them to get up and find people who can complete the tasks in the boxes and initial them. Set a time limit of about 10 to 12 minutes, depending on the size of the group. Keep reminding them of how much time is left.

To increase motivation, you might have prizes for the first one, two, or three to get bingo. When the game is over, ask the participants to discuss in pairs or in groups how they could use a similar activity with their own students.

This would also be an appropriate time to clarify any confusion, misconceptions, or uncertainties that may have arisen when the participants were answering the questions in the bingo grid.

Journal Writing

What are some advantages and disadvantages of teaching students to do lattice multiplication?

Preadolescent Brain Bingo Game Sheet

Directions: In this activity, the entire group gets up and moves around. Each person tries to find someone who can answer one of the questions in the box. The person who answers the question initials the box. The object is to get a bingo pattern (horizontally, vertically, or diagonally). No person may initial the same sheet twice. Time limit: 15 to 20 minutes, depending on the size of the group.

Find a person who is able to:

Explain what is meant by "number sense"	Describe two factors that hinder the use of technology	Explain what effective practice includes	Describe factors that influence the growing brain	Describe a strategy for developing number sense
Explain the purpose of number knowledge tests	Explain if multitasking shortens attention span	Describe an estimation activity	Discuss testing as a form of practice	Describe the role of graphic organizers
Explain the problem students have with the equal sign	Describe two factors that encourage use of technology	Discuss the development of the limbic area and frontal lobes	Give three ways of using technology in instruction	Explain the declarative-based approach to instruction
Describe the brain's gray matter	Explain the value of modeling	Describe two types of estimation	Explain cognitive closure	Explain what are "process skills"
Describe the functions of the limbic area	Explain what is meant by "novelty"	Discuss mathematical reasoning	Explain "teach for understanding"	Describe the brain's white matter

Chapter 6. Teaching Mathematics to the Adolescent Brain

Summary

- One of the functions of working memory is to control and guide voluntary behavior. Working memory is still developing in adolescents. Thus, adolescents are not as efficient as adults in recruiting areas that support working memory. Investigations of spatial working memory showed that early adolescents performed well on spatial working-memory tests, but they needed to engage more neural circuits than older adolescents.

- Older adolescents seem to recruit fewer neurons and use different strategies to perform the same job than younger adolescents. Researchers found that the older teens solved the task through a verbal strategy, rather than by rote spatial rehearsal. As adolescents mature, the brain uses more areas in general and distributes certain tasks to specialized regions. This process reduces the total neural effort necessary to achieve the same level of performance.

- When encountering a novel situation for which the individual has developed no coping strategy, the right hemisphere is primarily involved and attempts to deal with the situation. In mathematics, for instance, that could be the student's first encounter with solving quadratic equations. With repeated exposure to similar situations, coping strategies eventually emerge and learning occurs because it results in a change of behavior. In time, and after sufficient repetition, the responses become routine and shift to the left hemisphere. The amount of time and the number of situational exposures needed to accomplish this right-to-left hemisphere transition vary widely from one person to the next. But it may be that one component of mathematical aptitude is the ability of a student's brain to make right-to-left transitions involving mathematical operations in less time and with fewer exposures than average.

- Teachers ultimately decide whether mathematics is full or devoid of novelty. If adolescents have already mastered a mathematical operation, yet we continue to give them more of the same assignments, they see no purpose in completing repetitive practice. They lose interest, they see mathematics as boring and humdrum work, their motivation drops, and their grades slump. The key here is for the teacher to find different and meaningful applications of the mathematical operation or concept to maintain interest and attention, key components of motivation. Novelty and motivation are also undermined by a mathematics curriculum that focuses mainly on a strict formal approach, heavy in memorizing abstract axioms and theorems.

- One curious finding from fMRI studies is that adolescents could have an advantage over adults when learning algebra. The studies indicate that after several days of practice, adolescents, like adults, rely on the prefrontal cortex regions for retrieving algebraic rules to solve equations. However, unlike adults, after practice, adolescents decrease their reliance on the brain's parietal region that is holding an image of the equation. Compared with the adult brain, the developing prefrontal regions of the adolescent brain are more plastic and thus change more with practice, resulting in an enhanced ability for learning algebra.

- Cognitive researchers suggest that adolescent students approach the study of mathematics with different learning styles that run along a continuum from primarily quantitative to primarily qualitative. Students with a quantitative style approach mathematics in a linear, routinelike fashion. They prefer working with numbers over concrete models and may run into difficulty with solutions requiring multistep procedures. On the other hand, students with a qualitative style prefer concepts over routine steps and models over numbers. The implication is that students are more likely to be successful in learning mathematics if teachers use instructional strategies that are compatible with their students' cognitive styles, but that exposure to both kinds of strategies can strengthen a student's weakness.

- Inductive and deductive reasoning are among the most common types of reasoning used in mathematics. Inductive reasoning, sometimes called the bottom-up approach, moves from parts to a whole or from the specific to the general. In inductive reasoning, we begin with specific observations and measures, look for patterns and regularities, formulate some tentative hypotheses that we can explore, and develop general conclusions or theories. In deductive reasoning, sometimes called the top-down approach, one draws a conclusion from principles that are already known or hypothesized. Inductive reasoning is often used to make a guess at a property, and deductive reasoning is then used to prove that the property must hold for all cases, or for some set of cases.

- The layered curriculum approach developed by Kathie Nunley helps teachers in brain-compatible classrooms accomplish three basic goals: first, to increase student motivation by engaging students emotionally in their learning; second, to enable students to master mathematics skills to a level of proficiency that allows practical use of the skill, thus creating meaning; and third, to encourage higher-level thinking and to connect new learning to prior knowledge in a complex manner. Engaging students is first and foremost, because without engagement and motivation, teachers cannot begin to address the other two goals. Improving motivation and engagement in students requires only that teachers add one simple thing to their classroom—choice.

- Even students who are proficient at solving mathematical expressions can have difficulty interpreting the meaning of word problems. Authors of mathematics texts do not always follow the principles of writing that students have learned in their language arts classes. For example, students learn that an author's main idea usually appears in the passage's opening sentences. In mathematics problems, however, the main idea often appears in the last sentence. Teachers can help students interpret word problems by using strategies designed to focus on what the problem is asking and to select a solution, such as the SQRQCQ process (see page 155 in the text).

Supplemental Information

Research studies show that mathematics lessons in the United States often focus mainly on procedure instead of engaging students in exploring mathematics concepts. Teachers need to move beyond these ineffective teaching routines, and some researchers recommend braiding together mathematics, language, and cognition. Both reading comprehension and mathematics are based on cognitive strategies, including making connections, asking questions, visualizing, inferring, predicting, determining importance, and synthesizing.

One process recommended by Arthur Hyde (see the November 2007 issue of *Educational Leadership*, pages 43–47) is to modify the K-W-L strategy used in reading comprehension. This strategy focuses on three questions: What do I *know*? What do I *want* to learn more about? and What did I *learn*? In mathematics, this can be adapting to a K-W-C strategy: What do I *know* for sure? What do I *want* to find out? and Are there any special *conditions* that I have to watch for? Infusing language and thought into mathematics instruction may help to make it more meaningful to the adolescent brain.

Graphic organizers are known to be extremely helpful for students who have difficulty understanding the relationships between mathematical quantities. There are several Internet sites described in the **Resources** section of the text that are full of different types of graphic organizers. Encourage teachers at all grade levels to review the examples on pages 150–154 of the text and to seek out more on the Internet.

A major area of concern for adolescents is that they are not getting enough sleep. Adequate sleep is critical for mental and physical health. The encoding of information into the long-term memory sites occurs during sleep. When we sleep, the brain reviews the events and tasks of the day, storing them more securely than at the time we originally processed them. Thus, adequate sleep is vital to the memory storage process, especially for young learners. Most teenagers need eight to nine hours of sleep each night, but only about 20 percent are actually getting that amount. Several factors are responsible for eroding sleep time. In the morning, high schools start earlier, teens spend more time grooming, and some travel long distances to school. At the end of the day, there are athletic and social events, part-time jobs, homework, television, and video games. Add to this the shift in teens' body clocks that tends to keep them up later, and the average sleep time is more like five to six hours.

The problem is becoming so prevalent in middle and high schools that some neuroscientists and psychiatrists are convinced that it is a chronic disorder of the adolescent population. Called Delayed Sleep Phase Disorder (DSPD), it is characterized by a persistent pattern that includes difficulty falling asleep at night and getting up in the morning, fatigue during the day, and alertness at night. Caused mainly by the shift in the adolescent's sleep-wake cycle, DSPD is aggravated by other conditions, such as anxiety and too much caffeine.

Most of the encoding of information and skills into long-term storage is believed to occur during the rapid-eye movement (REM) phases. During the normal sleep time of eight to nine hours, five REM cycles occur. Adolescents getting just five to six hours of sleep lose out on the last two REM cycles, thereby reducing the amount of time the brain has to consolidate information and skills into long-term storage. This sleep deprivation not only disturbs the memory storage process, but it puts the body under stress and can lead to other problems as well. Students may nod off in class or become irritable. Worse, their decreased alertness due to fatigue can lead to accidents in school and in their cars.

Students who get less sleep are more likely to get poorer grades in school than students who sleep longer. Sleep-deprived students also had more daytime sleepiness, depressed moods, and behavioral problems. It is important that educators and parents remind students of the significance of sleep to their mental and physical health and to encourage them to reexamine their daily activities to provide for adequate sleep.

Discussion Questions

1. Explain the development of working memory in the adolescent brain.
2. Describe how the brain deals with novel and routine experiences.
3. What implications does the brain's search for novelty have for teaching and learning mathematics?
4. What are some of the mathematical behaviors of learners with quantitative style?
5. What are some of the mathematical behaviors of learners with qualitative style?
6. Explain the difference between inductive and deductive reasoning.
7. What are the three steps in the layered curriculum approach?
8. What are some advantages to using graphic organizers in teaching mathematics? Are there any disadvantages?
9. Describe the SQRQCQ process.
10. What are some specific ways that teachers can make mathematics meaningful to teenagers?

Activity

- *Planning a Layered Curriculum Unit*

Time: 30–35 minutes, with reading
Materials: Chart paper, markers, *How the Brain Learns Mathematics*

The purpose of this activity is to give the participants some practice in designing a teaching unit using Kathie Nunley's successful approach known as layering the curriculum. This activity goes faster if the participants have already read pages 143–148 of the text.

Divide the participants into groups of four or five by similar grade levels. For example, you might have smaller groups divided into middle school and high school. Larger groups could be divided by grade levels, if there are enough to make a reasonable group. Give each group a few sheets of chart paper and markers, and ask them to select a recorder.

Tell them that they will have about 10 minutes to silently read (or review) pages 143–148 of the text. When the reading is completed, the group's task is to select a topic in mathematics appropriate to their grade level(s) and to outline a layered curriculum unit for that topic. They will have about 20 minutes for this task. The recorder should write down the outline on the chart paper.

When time is up, each recorder (or selected recorders, if there is a large number of groups) briefly describes the unit to the entire group.

Journal Writing

What advantages are there to using the layered curriculum approach? Any disadvantages?

Chapter 7. Recognizing and Addressing Mathematics Difficulties

Summary

- The percentage of school-age children who experience difficulties in learning mathematics has been growing steadily. Why is that? The answer to this question is complicated by at least two considerations. First, we need to distinguish whether the poor achievement is due to inadequate instruction or some other environmental factor, or whether it is due to an actual cognitive disability. Second, exactly how is mathematics being taught? Instructional approaches can determine whether a cognitive deficit is really a disability at all. For example, one instructional approach emphasizes conceptual understanding, but another approach places heavy emphasis on procedures and facts. A student with a deficit in retrieving arithmetic facts might not be considered as having a learning disability in the first approach because of the de-emphasis on memory-based information. However, that deficit would be a serious disability in the second approach.

- In this chapter, the term *mathematics difficulties* includes those students performing in the low average range, regardless of whether their difficulties are due to environmental factors or cognitive deficits. It is important to remember that because mathematics achievement tests include many types of items, it is possible that students may demonstrate average performance in some areas of mathematics and show deficits in other areas.

- The first task facing educators who deal with students with mathematics difficulties is to determine the nature of the problem. Obviously, environmental causes require different interventions than developmental causes. Low performance on a mathematics test *may* indicate that a problem exists, but tests do not provide information on the exact source of the poor performance.

- Teachers in the primary grades often rely on their own observations of students' performance to determine when a particular child is having problems with arithmetic computations. Although teacher observations are valuable, other measures should be considered as well. Research studies have shown that several measures are reliable in detecting and predicting how well young students are mastering number manipulation and basic arithmetic operations.

- Past the primary grades, research studies over the past 15 years suggest that five critical factors affect the learning of mathematics. Each factor can serve as a diagnostic tool for assessing the nature of any learning difficulties students may experience with mathematical processing. The factors are level of cognitive awareness, mathematics learning profile, language of mathematics, prerequisite skills, and levels of learning mastery.

- Math anxiety is a feeling of tension that interferes with the manipulations of numbers and the solving of mathematical problems in academic and ordinary life situations. Some studies suggest that more than 60 percent of adults have a fear of mathematics. Students at all grade levels often develop a fear (or phobia) of mathematics because of negative experiences in their past or current mathematics class or have a simple lack of self-confidence with numbers. In people with math anxiety, the fear of failure often causes their minds to draw a blank. Added pressure of having time limits on mathematics tests also raises the level of anxiety for many students. Students with this phobia have a limited understanding of mathematical concepts. They may rely mainly on memorizing procedures, rules, and routines without much conceptual understanding. Regardless of the source, the most prevalent consequences of this anxiety are poor achievement and poor grades in mathematics.

- Five areas appear to contribute in one way or another to math anxiety: teachers' attitudes, curriculum, instructional strategies, the classroom culture, and assessment.

- About 5 to 8 percent of school-age students have serious difficulty processing mathematics. This condition, referred to as *dyscalculia*, is a difficulty in conceptualizing numbers, number relationships, outcomes of numerical operations, and estimation, that is, what to expect as an outcome of an operation. If the condition is present from birth, it is called *developmental dyscalculia*. Genetic studies reveal that developmental dyscalculia is inheritable. If the condition results from an injury to the brain after birth, it is called *acquired dyscalculia*. Whether developmental or acquired, for most individuals, this disorder is the result of specific disabilities in basic numerical processing and not the consequence of deficits in other cognitive abilities.

- Other mathematical disorders include number concept difficulties, counting skill deficits, difficulties with arithmetic skills, procedural disorders, memory disorders, and visual-spatial deficits. Dyscalculia can be associated with reading disorders, attention-deficit hyperactivity disorder (ADHD), and nonverbal learning disability.

- Students who have difficulties with mathematics can benefit significantly from lessons that include multiple models that approach a concept at different cognitive levels, such as the concrete-pictorial-abstract, or the CPA, approach. Concrete components include manipulatives, measuring tools, or other objects the students can handle during the lesson. Pictorial representations include drawings, diagrams, charts, or graphs that are drawn by the students or are provided for the students to read and interpret. Abstract refers to symbolic representations, such as numbers or letters, that the student writes or interprets to demonstrate understanding of a task.

- When using the CPA approach, the sequencing of activities is critical. Activities with concrete materials should come first to impress on students that mathematical operations can be used to solve real-world problems. Pictured relationships show visual representations of the concrete manipulatives and help students visualize mathematical operations during problem solving. It is important here that the teacher explain how the pictorial examples relate to the concrete examples. Finally, formal work with symbols is used to demonstrate how symbols provide a shorter and efficient way to represent numerical operations. Ultimately, students need to reach that final abstract level by using symbols proficiently with many of the mathematical skills they master.

- This CPA approach benefits all students but has been shown to be particularly effective with students who have mathematics difficulties, mainly because it moves gradually from actual objects through pictures and then to symbols. These students often get frustrated when teachers present mathematics problems only in the abstract.

- A process mnemonic is designed to help remember rules, principles, and procedures. Process mnemonics serve to recall the orderly cognitive processes required in problem solving. They are useful when teaching the computational skills of addition, subtraction, multiplication, and division, and for remembering rules and procedures in spelling, trigonometry, mathematics, and science. Process mnemonics incorporate vivid images, such as representing mathematical rules with more memorable phrases. Sentences, phrases, songs, and rhymes are used to teach the steps in solving the problems. The components of computation are explained in elaborate stories, and the concepts are explained through things familiar to students, such as warriors, joggers, swimmers, and bugs. Process mnemonics are so effective with students who have mathematics difficulties because they are powerful memory devices that actively engage the brain in processes fundamental to learning and memory. They incorporate meaning through metaphors that are relevant to today's students, they are attention getting and motivating, and they use visualization techniques that help students link concrete associations with abstract symbols.

- Students who have both reading and mathematics difficulties are obviously at a double disadvantage. However, even though the reading and mathematical processing areas of the brain are separate from each other, these two cerebral regions interact whenever the learner must translate word problems into symbolic representations. Effective strategies include using cue words in word problems, word problem maps, and the RIDD strategy (see page 193 in the text).

Supplemental Information

Recent studies have shown that some boys who have difficulties in algebra are really having trouble translating word problems into algebraic expressions. When given just the equations, most boys were able to solve the expressions correctly. Researchers suggest that teachers should spend much more time teaching mathematics as a second language, so students understand its unique terminology, syntax, and other linguistic elements.

Although dyscalculia can be associated in the same individual with other learning disorders, most dyscalculia is the result of specific disabilities in the numerical processing areas of the brain, rather than of deficits in other cognitive abilities. Thus, teachers and parents should not assume that students who have difficulty with mathematics will also have difficulty in other curriculum areas.

Discussion Questions

1. Discuss the prerequisite skills associated with learning mathematics.

2. What five factors need to be considered when assessing postprimary mathematical skills?
3. What are some of the diagnostic tools used for assessing learning difficulties in mathematics?
4. What are some of the causes of math anxiety?
5. What are some ways to alleviate math anxiety in the classroom?
6. What is dyscalculia and what are its symptoms?
7. What are some of the types of dyscalculia?
8. With what other disorders is dyscalculia associated?
9. Describe the concrete-pictorial-abstract approach to teaching mathematics.
10. Explain process mnemonics.
11. What are some strategies that can help students who have both reading and mathematics difficulties?

Activity

● *Alleviating Math Anxiety*

Time: 20 minutes
Materials: Self-Assessment on Alleviating Math Anxiety Form

Math anxiety continues to plague the student population. At a time when we need more students learning all levels of mathematics, teachers need to assess their classroom climate and instructional choices to ensure that they keep the factors that contribute to math anxiety to a minimum.

This activity is for teachers of mathematics at all grade levels and their supervisors. It is designed as a simple self-assessment of some of the decisions they make in the classroom. In order to obtain valid responses from the participants, ensure them that they will **not** be asked to share their assessment with anyone else.

Give a copy of the assessment form (see page 36 on this guide) to each participant, and tell them they have about 6 minutes to complete it. (Give them more time if they need it. It is important that everyone complete the assessment.) Remind them to be candid, that their first response is probably the most valid, and that they should not dwell on any one statement. When they are done, ask them to connect the circles with straight lines. This yields a graphic profile of their responses. Now ask them to reflect on the question at the bottom of the assessment sheet and to answer the "Journal Writing" question in their journals.

Ask if any of the participants would like to make a comment or suggestion for the entire group to discuss.

Journal Writing

What are three things that I will purposefully do (or continue to do) to alleviate math anxiety in my classroom?

Self-Assessment on Alleviating Math Anxiety Form

Directions: On a scale of 1 (lowest) to 5 (highest), circle the number that indicates the degree to which each statement **generally** reflects your classroom practice.

	5	4	3	2	1
I show how mathematics contributes to other disciplines	5	4	3	2	1
I assign tasks that are relevant to students	5	4	3	2	1
I focus on the process of learning rather than searching for just the correct answer	5	4	3	2	1
I create opportunities for success in my assignments	5	4	3	2	1
I resist the notion that males have a greater innate aptitude in mathematics than females	5	4	3	2	1
I display subject-matter confidence in my teaching	5	4	3	2	1
I often provide opportunities that allow students to use mathematics as a tool for discovery	5	4	3	2	1
I eliminate less important items from the curriculum in order to get a deeper understanding of major topics	5	4	3	2	1
I can detect when students are confused or frustrated	5	4	3	2	1
I pose questions to help students continuously learn rather than to catch them being wrong	5	4	3	2	1
I limit the frequency of memorizing and rote practice	5	4	3	2	1
I usually show a practical application of the mathematical concept they are learning	5	4	3	2	1
I use projects that allow students to explore solutions to problems individually and in groups	5	4	3	2	1
I maintain a climate where students feel at ease asking questions and exploring ideas	5	4	3	2	1
I discourage valuing speed over time for reflection	5	4	3	2	1
I encourage students to make sense of what they are learning rather than memorizing steps and procedures	5	4	3	2	1

Connect the circles to see a profile. What action might you take regarding any responses that are "1" or "2"? _____

_____

Chapter 8. Putting It All Together: Planning Lessons in PreK–12 Mathematics

Summary

- Mathematics can be described as the study of all possible patterns. Patterns include order, structure, and logical relationships and go beyond the visual patterns found in tiles and wallpaper to patterns that occur everywhere in nature. Some patterns are numerical and can be described with numbers, such as voting patterns of a nation or the odds of winning the lottery. But other patterns are visual designs that are not connected to numbers at all.

- If mathematics is the science of patterns that exist all around us, then mathematics is not just about numbers but about the world we live in. If that is the case, then why are so many students turned off by mathematics and have the impression that mathematics is a sterile subject filled with meaningless abstract symbols? Educators have to work harder at planning a mathematics curriculum that is exciting and relevant and at designing lessons that carry this excitement into every day's instruction.

- After deciding a lesson's content objective, one of the next steps is to design the learning episode. Questions to keep in mind while planning for effective instruction are: Is the lesson memory-compatible? Does the lesson include cognitive closure? Will the primacy-recency effect be taken into account? What kind of practice will occur? What writing will be involved? Are multiple intelligences being addressed? and Does the lesson provide for differentiation?

- A reasonable model for teaching mathematics to children and adolescents would proceed through four major steps. The first step would be to build on young children's intuitions about numbers, subitizing, quantitative manipulations, and counting. These innate talents are strongly rooted in developing neural networks and should be cultivated with concrete activities rather than stunted with paper worksheets.

- The next step is to introduce them to symbolic notation in mathematics, emphasizing how it offers a powerful and convenient shortcut when manipulating quantities. It is important at this point to continue to tie the symbolic knowledge once again to the quantitative intuitions. In this way, the symbolic representations become part of the intuitive network instead of being memorized as a separate and unrelated language.

- In step three, introduce the preadolescent brain to arithmetic axioms. Appropriate concrete manipulatives should be used here as much as possible because we are moving into that critical time when students can be turned off by the increasingly abstract nature of symbolic mathematics. Later, as adolescents, their brain's frontal lobe becomes more adept at higher-order thinking and logic.

- In step four, introduce and explain mathematical and geometric axioms and theorems. But it is still necessary to show practical applications whenever possible. Remember, when students understand and recognize practical uses for what they are learning, they can attach meaning and thus increase their chances of retention.

- This model may be simplistic. On the other hand, one reason that students get turned off to mathematics is that we often do not try hard enough to keep relating what they are experiencing in the classroom to concrete and practical applications. There are few school subjects in which teachers hear the lament, "Why do I have to know this?" more than in mathematics. That observation alone should be ample warning that we have to work harder at meaning.

Supplemental Information

The model for PreK–12 mathematics instruction shown in this chapter (Figure 8.2, page 214) is by no means *the* final word on how and when to teach mathematical concepts. But it is based on the research in cognitive psychology and cognitive neuroscience about how and when the developing human brain deals with numbers and mathematical relationships. It has passed the critical peer review of both researchers and practitioners.

At the very least, the model should spark a lively discussion among participants who are involved in mathematics education. I have intentionally not included here a specific activity focusing on a discussion of the model. Rather, because of its multiple implications, I have left it to the facilitator to decide on the best format for such a discussion.

Discussion Questions

1. Discuss your view of the statement, "Mathematics is the science of patterns."
2. What are some of the instructional questions that teachers should ask themselves when planning lessons?
3. What are some strategies for using writing in mathematics?
4. Describe Gardner's eight multiple intelligences.
5. What are some ways that teachers can differentiate lessons?
6. Describe the author's four-step instructional model for PreK–12 mathematics instruction.

Activity

● *Planning an Activity for Multiple Intelligences*

Time: 25–30 minutes, including reading time
Materials: Chart paper, marking pens, *How the Brain Learns Mathematics*

The purpose of this activity is to have the participants think about lesson techniques that address each of the eight intelligences proposed by Howard Gardner. The activity goes faster if the participants have already read pages 208–209.

Divide the participants into groups of four or five by similar grade levels. For example, you might have smaller groups divided into middle school and high school. Larger groups could be divided by grade levels, if there are enough to make a reasonable group. Give each group a few sheets of chart paper and markers, and ask them to select a recorder.

Tell them that they will have about 10 minutes to silently read (or review) pages 208–209 of the text. When the reading is completed, the group's task is to select a lesson topic in mathematics appropriate to their grade level(s) and to suggest activities for each of Gardner's eight intelligences shown in Table 8.1. They will have about 20 minutes for this task. The recorder should write down the outline on the chart paper.

When time is up, each recorder (or selected recorders, if there is a large number of groups) briefly describes one activity from each of the intelligences.

Journal Writing

In what ways can addressing multiple intelligences improve teaching and learning in my classroom?

Workshop Evaluation Form

- How well did the seminar meet the goals and objectives?

- How will you apply what you learned during this seminar in your daily professional life?

- What professional support will you need to implement what you have learned from this seminar?

- How well did the topics explored in this seminar meet a specific need in your school or district?

- How relevant was this topic to your professional life?

Process

- How well did the instructional techniques and activities facilitate your understanding of the topic?

- How can you incorporate the activities learned today into your daily professional life?

- Were a variety of learning experiences included in the seminar?

- Was any particular activity memorable? What made it stand out?

Context

- Were the facilities conducive to learning?

- Were the accommodations adequate for the activities involved?

Overall

- Overall, how successful would you consider this seminar? Please include a brief comment or explanation.

- What was the most valuable thing you gained from this seminar experience?

Additional Comments

SOURCE: Adapted from *Evaluating Professional Development* by Thomas R. Guskey, Corwin Press, 2000.

Notes

CORWIN PRESS

The Corwin Press logo—a raven striding across an open book—represents the union of courage and learning. Corwin Press is committed to improving education for all learners by publishing books and other professional development resources for those serving the field of PreK–12 education. By providing practical, hands-on materials, Corwin Press continues to carry out the promise of its motto: **"Helping Educators Do Their Work Better."**

Printed in the United States
By Bookmasters